OUR DAY OUT

Originally written as a television play and transmitted as a BBC "Play for Today" in 1976. Subsequently adapted for the stage and first performed at the Everyman Theatre, Liverpool, on 8 April 1983, with the following cast:

Mrs Kay	Linda Beckett
Bus Driver/Zoo Keeper/Les	Carl Chase
Colin/Headmaster	David Hobbs
Mr Briggs	Robert McIntosh
Susan/Café Owner	Christina Nagy

The Children

*X Company:** Sue Abrahams, Michaela Amoo, Danny Ayers, Maria Barrett, Angela Bell, Andy Broadhead, Maxine Cole, Vernon Eustace, Brian Hanlon, Michael Kagbo, Andrea Langham, Victor McGuire, Mary Shepherd, Paul Spencer, Charlie Thelu, Jason Williams
*Y Company:** Hannah Bond, Peter Bullock, Shaun Carr, Mary Farmer, Danny Jones, Anne Lundon, Ritchie Macauley, Keith Maiker, Jacqui McCarthy, Victor McGuire, Jocelyn Meall, Joanne Mogan, Joanne Oldham, Joanne Pennington, Ben Wilson, John Winstanley

*X and Y performed on alternative nights

Directed by Bob Eaton and Kate Roland
Musical direction by Chris Mellor
Designed by Sue Mayes
Lighting designed by Kevin Fitzsimons

Subsequently seen at the Young Vic Theatre, London, from 20 August 1983, with the following cast:

Mrs Kay	Rosalind Boxall
Bus Driver/Zoo Keeper/Les	Martin Stone
Colin/Headmaster	William Gaminara
Mr Briggs	Stephen Lewis
Susan/Café Owner	Christina Nagy

The Children: Matthew Barker, Paul Billings, Gillian Blavo, Maura Hall, Michelle Bristol, Richard Cotterill, Brian Warrington, Tony Fuller, Jane Gibbs, Claire Mitchell, Paul Harbert, Roy Spicer, Sally Hobbs, Tony Jones, Darragh Murray, Darryl Niven, Marie Quetant, Jason Robertson, Jaqueline Rodger, Elizabeth Toone

Directed by Bob Eaton
Musical direction by Stuart Barham
Designed by Sue Mayes
Lighting by Andy Phillips

[7|10|03}
3m 2F

Our Day Out

A Play with music

Willy Russell

Songs and music by Bob Eaton, Chris Mellor and Willy Russell

Samuel French - London
New York - Toronto - Hollywood

MUSICAL NUMBERS

ACT I

Song

1	We're Going Out	Carol and the Kids
2	Mrs Kay's Progress Class	Kids
2(a)	Got A Packed Lunch	Kids
3	Boss of the Bus	Driver
4	Instructions on Enjoyment	Mr Briggs
5	We're Off	Kids
6	Look At The Dogs	Kids
7	The Mersey Tunnel	Kids
8	Straight Line	Mr Briggs and Mrs Kay
9	Penny Chews	Kids
10	I'm In Love With Sir	Linda, Jackie and the Kids
11	Zoo Song (Who's Watching Who?)	Kids

ACT II

12	Castle Song	Mr Briggs, Colin, Jackie, Linda
12(a)	Beach Song	Kids
13	I Know You Like Her	Susan, Reilly
14	Why Can't It Always Be This Way?	Carol
15	Fairground Song	Company
16	Everywhere We Go	Kids
16(a)	We Had A Really Great Day Out	Kids
	No-One Can Take This Time Away	Kids

AUTHOR'S NOTE

Language and Setting

For the purpose of publication I have retained the play's original settings of Liverpool and Wales but this is not intended to imply that productions of the play in other parts of the country should strive to observe the original setting or reproduce the idiom in which it is written. If being played in, say, Sheffield, the play would, I feel, be more relevant to both cast and audience if adapted to a local setting and the local accent.

Following the play's original production in Liverpool it was staged at The Young Vic where it became a Cockney play; the setting of the school became Hackney, the Mersey Tunnel became the Blackwall Tunnel, Conway Castle became Bodiam Castle, the Welsh Coast, the South Coast and so on.

I can foresee a problem where the play is set in an area which has no road tunnel or bridge and if this is the case, would suggest that you simply cut this small section of script.

Staging

Although it would be possible to present the play on a proscenium stage I think it's much better suited to a more flexible area. The play was originally presented in the round, with a set that consisted of a number of simple benches. These benches were used as the seats on the coach and then re-arranged by the actors to suggest the various other settings—the café, the zoo, even the rocks on the beach.

Two platforms were built at a higher level and were used as the castle battlements, the cliff and the headmaster's study.

In both the Everyman and Young Vic productions the coach carried about fifteen to twenty passengers. Obviously this number could be increased for large cast productions.

Music

Again, in the original productions of the play the production budgets demanded that the musical accompaniment be kept to an absolute minimum—i.e. piano and percussion. Should you be in the happy position of knowing no such constraints and have at your disposal a band or orchestra, please feel free to arrange the music accordingly.

The score is available on hire from Samuel French Ltd.

Willy Russell

ACT I

As the musical introduction for Song 1 is heard, Les, the lollipop man, enters. He is very old, almost blind and can hardly walk

A group of kids, on their way to school, enter, shouting "Hi-ya, Les" and "All right, Les". They sing

Song 1: We're Goin' Out

Kids
We're goin' out
Just for the day
Goin' off somewhere far away
Out to the country
Maybe to the sea
Me Mam says I can go ... if it's free

During the next verse the kids exit, singing

Carol enters, singing

Carol ⎫ *(together)*
Kids ⎭
The sky is blue
The sun's gonna shine
Better hurry up cos it's nearly nine
This is the day that's
Just for us
We're goin' out ... on a bus

Carol is about to make her way to the school when she notices Les on the other side of the road

Carol Hi-ya, Les.
Les *(peering)* Who's that?
Carol *(crossing to Les)* Carol, it's Carol, Les.
Les Hello, love. 'Ey, can y' see me back across the road?

Carol takes his arm and leads him back

You're early today aren't you?
Carol Yeh. We're goin' out. On a trip.
Les Where to?
Carol I dunno. It's somewhere far away. I forget.
Les Are they all goin'?

Carol Only the kids in the Progress Class.

Les The what?

Carol Don't y'know what the Progress Class is? It's Mrs Kay's class. Y' go down there in the week if y' can't do readin' or sums or writin'. If you're backward like.

Les By Christ, I'll bet she's kept busy. They're all bloody backward round here.

Carol I know. I better be goin' now, Les. I'm gonna be late. An' there's Briggs!

Mr Briggs is seen approaching

Les (*calling to Carol*) Ta-rah, girl. Mind how you go.

Carol (*running off*) See y', Les.

Carol exits

Briggs is about to cross the road when Les calls to him

Les 'Ey, you! Don't move.

Briggs I beg your pardon.

Les Wait. There.

Briggs Look, I've not got the time to ...

Les No one crosses the road without the assistance of the lollipop man, no one.

Briggs Look, man ...

Les The Government hired me!

Briggs But there's nothing coming.

Les How do you know? How do you know a truck or a car isn't gonna come speedin' out of them side roads? Eh? How can you set an example to kids if you're content to walk under the wheels of a juggernaut?

Les goes to the centre of the road and waves Briggs across

That's why the Government hires me!

Mrs Kay and the Kids enter

Song 2: Mrs Kay's Progress Class

Kids (*singing*)   Mis-ses Kay's Progress Class
We're the ones who
Never pass
We're goin' out
Off with Mis-ses Kay
We're goin' out. ... today

Mrs Kay All right all right. Will you just let me have a bit of peace and I'll get you *all* sorted out. Right, now look (*spelling it out*) all those who've got permission to come on the trip, but who haven't yet paid, I want you to come over here.

She separates herself from the group. Every kid follows her. Briggs passes and surveys the scene with obvious disapproval

Mrs Kay (*brightly*) 'Morning, Mr Briggs.
Briggs (*grudgingly*) 'Morning.

As Briggs turns towards the school a couple of kids emerge

Briggs Come on, you two. Where are you supposed to be? Move!

The boys rush to the safety of Mrs Kay's group

  Briggs exits

Song 2a: Got a Packed Lunch
Kids

  (*singing, as a round*)   Got a packed lunch
                            Got money to spend
                            Gonna get a seat near my best friend
                            Just can't wait to get
                            Away from here
                            Gonna bring me Mam—a souvenir

As the round ends there is a Black-Out, during which the Kids re-arrange the benches to form the coach

  The Lights come up on the Headmaster's study as Briggs enters

Briggs When was this arranged?
Headmaster Don't talk to me about it. After the last trip of hers I said "no more", absolutely no more. Look, just look. (*He indicates a file*) Complaints from the residents of Derbyshire.
Briggs Well, how the hell's she arranged this then?
Headmaster When I was away at conference. George approved it in my absence. He wasn't aware of any ban on remedial department outings.
Briggs It'll have to be cancelled.
Headmaster If it is she'll resign.
Briggs Good. The school would be better off without her.
Headmaster There's not many of her type about y' know. By and

large I reckon she does a good job. She keeps them well out of the way with their reading machines and plasticine. It's just when she gets let loose with them.

Briggs OK. I'll have to go with her, won't I?

The Lights go down on the study and come up on Mrs Kay talking to a young teacher, Susan. Around them are lively excited kids in random groups. Two kids are pulling and pushing each other

Mrs Kay Maurice! Come away from that road!

Maurice I'm sorry, Miss.

Mrs Kay Come on, keep on the side where it's safe.

Two older kids, aged about fifteen (Reilly and Digga), come rushing out of school and approach the teachers

Reilly Ey, Miss, hang on, hang on. Can we come with y' Miss. Can we?

Digga Go on Miss, don't be tight, let's come.

Reilly Go on Miss, say yeh.

Mrs Kay Brian, you know it's a trip for the Progress Class.

Reilly Yeh, well, we used to be in the Progress Class didn't we?

Susan But Brian, you're not in the Progress Class any longer are you? Now that you can read and write you're back in normal classes.

Reilly Ah, Miss, come on.

Mrs Kay Brian, you know that I'd willingly take you, but it's not up to me. Who's your form teacher?

Reilly Briggsy.

Mrs Kay Well, I'll take you, if you get his permission.

Reilly Ooh, you're sound, Miss.

Reilly and Digga begin to run off

Mrs Kay Brian!

Reilly and Digga stop

Bring a note.

Reilly Ah, Miss, what for?

Mrs Kay Because I wasn't born yesterday and if I don't ask you to bring a note you'll just hide behind that wall for two minutes and then tell me Mr Briggs gave permission.

Reilly As if we'd do something like that, Miss.

Mrs Kay I want it in writing.

Reilly and Digga exit

Carol (*tugging at Mrs Kay's arm*) Where we goin' eh, Miss?

Mrs Kay Carol! Miss Duncan's just told you; Conway, we're going to Conway.

Carol Is that in England, Miss?

Susan It's in Wales, Carol.

Carol Will we have to get a boat?

Colin enters, running

Colin Sorry I'm late. Car wouldn't start.

Linda Hi-ya, Sir.

Jackie Hi-ya, Sir.

Colin Hello, girls. (*Avoiding them—or trying to*) Erm, Mrs Kay . . .

Linda Sir, I thought for a minute you weren't comin' on the trip. I was heart-broken.

Colin Yes, erm . . . er . . .

Carol Miss, how will we get there?

Mrs Kay Carol! We're going on a coach. Look, here. (*Shouting to all the kids*) You can get on now. Go on . . .

There is a wild rush of kids to the coach

Suddenly the driver is there, blocking their way

Driver Right. Just stop there. No one move!

Kid Miss said we could get on.

Driver Oh, did she now?

Kids Yeh.

Driver Well, let me tell youse lot somethin' now. Miss is not the driver of this bus. I am! An' if I say y' don't get on, y' don't get on.

(*Singing*)
>   **Song 3: Boss of the Bus**
>
>   This is my bus
>   I'm the boss of the bus
>   I've been drivin' it for fifteen years
>   This is my bus
>   I'm the boss of the bus
>   So just pin back your ears
>   I'm the number one
>   I'm the driver man
>   And you kids don't get on
>   Till I say you can

This is my bus
I'm the boss of the bus
And the lesson I want learned
This is my bus
I'm the boss of the bus
And as far as I'm concerned
If you wanna put
One over on me
You're gonna need a damn sight more
Than a G.C.E.

Don't want no lemonade, no sweets
Don't want no chewing gum
'Cos the bleedin' stuff gets stuck to the seats
And respectable passengers' bums

This is my bus
I'm the boss of the bus
And I've seen it all before
This is my bus
I'm the boss of the bus
And I don't want no spew on the floor
I don't want no mess
Don't want no fuss
So keep your dirty hands
From off of my bus.

This is my bus

Kids	He's the boss of the bus
Driver	This is my bus
Kids	He's the boss of the bus
Driver	This is my bus
Kids	He's the boss of the bus
Driver	This is my bus
Kids	He's the boss of the bus
	There's nothing wrong with us

Driver (*heaving off a kid who managed to get on to the bus*) Get off of my bus.

Mrs Kay Is there something the matter, Driver?

Driver Are these children in your charge, madam?

Mrs Kay Yes.

Driver Well, you haven't checked them have y'?

Mrs Kay Checked them? Checked them for what?

Driver Chocolate and lemonade! We don't allow it. I've seen it on other coaches madam; fifty-two vomittin' kids, it's no joke. I'm sorry, but we don't allow that.

Mrs Kay (*to Susan*) Here comes Mr Happiness. All right Driver, I'll check them for you. Now listen, everyone: if anyone has brought chocolate or lemonade with them I want them to put up their hands.

A sea of innocent faces and unraised hands

There you are Driver, all right?

Driver No, it's not right. Y' can't just take their word for it. They have to be searched. You can't just believe kids.

Pause. Mrs Kay could blow up but she doesn't

Mrs Kay Can I have a word with you, Driver, in private?

The Driver comes off the coach. She manoeuvres it so that the Driver has his back to the kids and other teachers

What's your name, Driver?

Driver Me name? I don't usually have to give me name.

Mrs Kay Oh, come on. What's your name?

Driver Schofield, Ronnie Schofield.

Mrs Kay Well, Ronnie (*pointing*), just take a look at those streets.

As the Driver looks Mrs Kay motions, behind his back, indicating that the other teachers should get the kids on to the coach

Ronnie, would you say they were the sort of streets that housed prosperous parents?

Driver We usually do the better schools.

Mrs Kay All right, you don't like these kids, I can see that. But do you really have to cause them so much pain?

Driver What have I said? I only told them to wait.

Mrs Kay Ronnie, the kids with me today don't know what it is to *look* at a bar of chocolate. Lemonade, Ronnie? Lemonade never touches their lips. (*We should almost hear the violins*) These are the children, Ronnie, that stand outside shop windows in the pouring rain, looking and longing, but never getting. Even at Christmas time, when your kids from the better schools are singing carols, opening presents, these kids are left outside, left to wander the cold cruel streets.

The Driver is grief-stricken. Behind him, in the coach the kids are stuffing themselves stupid with sweets, chocolate and lemonade. Mrs Kay leaves the Driver to it and climbs on board. As the Driver turns to board the coach all evidence of sweets and lemonade immediately disappears. The Driver puts his hand in his pocket and produces a few quid

Driver (*to a kid on the front seat*) Here y' are son, run to the shops an see what sweets y' can get with that.

Susan (*leaning across*) What did you say?

Mrs Kay Lied like hell, of course. (*She gets up and faces the kids*)

Mrs Kay Now, listen everyone. Listen. We'll be setting off for Conway in a couple of minutes.

Cheers from everyone

Listen. Now, we want everybody to enjoy themselves today and so I don't want any silly squabbling and I don't want anybody doing anything dangerous either to yourselves or to others. That's the only rule we're going to have today, think of yourselves, but think of others as well.

Reilly and Digga come rushing on to the coach

Reilly Miss, we're comin', Miss, we're comin' with y' . . .

Mrs Kay Where's the note, Brian?

Reilly He didn't give us one, Miss. He's comin' himself. He said to wait.

Reilly and Digga go down the aisle to the back of the coach

Colin He's coming to keep an eye on us.

Susan To make sure we don't enjoy ourselves.

Mrs Kay Well, I suppose we'll just have to deal with him the best way we can.

Mrs Kay sits down, next to Carol. Reilly and Digga go to the back seat

Reilly (*to a little kid on the back seat*) Right. You. Move.

Little Kid Why?

Reilly Cos we claimed the back seat, that's why.

Little Kid You're not even in the Progress, though.

Briggs gets on to the coach, unseen by Reilly and Digga

Digga 'Ey, hardfaced, we used to be, so shift!

Reilly Now move before I mince y'.

Briggs glares at the Kids. All the Kids spot a cloud on the blue horizon

Briggs (*barking, suddenly*) Reilly, Dickson sit down!
Reilly Sir, we was only ...
Briggs (*staccato*) I said sit, lad, now move.

Reilly and Digga sit on the little kid who is forced out. He stands, exposed in the aisle, terrified of Briggs

Briggs Sit down. What you doing, lad, what you doing?
Little Kid Sir, Sir, Sir. . . . Sir, I haven't got a seat. (*He is almost in tears*)
Briggs Well, find one, boy, find one!

Colin gets out of his seat and indicates to the kid to sit there

Briggs (*to Mrs Kay*) You've got some real bright sparks here, Mrs Kay. A right bunch.
Mrs Kay Well, I think we might just manage to survive now that you've come to look after us.
Briggs The boss thought it might be a good idea if you had an extra member of staff. Looking at this lot I'd say he was right. There's a few of them I could sling off right now. (*Barking*) Linda Croxley, what are you doin'? Sit down, girl. (*He addresses all the kids*) Right! Now listen:

The Introduction to Song 4 begins beneath the dialogue

We wouldn't like you to think that we don't want you to enjoy yourselves today, because we do. But a lot of you won't have been on a school outing before and therefore won't know *how* to enjoy yourselves. So I'll tell you:

Song 4: Instructions on Enjoyment
Briggs   To enjoy a trip upon a coach
(*singing*)   We sit upon our seats
                    We do not wander up and down the aisles
                    We do not use obscenities
                    Or throw each other sweets
                    We talk politely, quietly nod and smile.
(*Speaking*) There'll be no shouting on this outing, will there?
(*Screaming*) Will there?
Kids No, Sir.

Briggs No Sir, no Sir.
    (*Singing*)   We look nicely through the windows
                At the pretty scenery
                We do not raise our voices, feet or fists
                And I do not, are you listening, girl,
                I do not want to see
                Two fingers raised to passing motorists
                To enjoy this treat
    (*Speaking*) Just stay in your seat
    Be quiet, be good and behave!

As Briggs finishes the song the kid who went to get the sweets rushes on board loaded with bags

Kid I've got them. I've got loads.
Briggs Where've you been?
Kid Sir, gettin' sweets.
Briggs Sweets? SWEETS!
Mrs Kay (*reaching for the sweets*) Thank you, Maurice.

The Driver taps Briggs on the shoulder

Driver Can I have a word with you?
Briggs Pardon.
Driver In private.

The Driver leads the way off the coach. Briggs follows. Mrs Kay gives the sweets to Colin and Susan who start to dish them out

Kids (*variously*) 'Ooh, great', 'Give us one, Miss,' 'What about me, Sir?'
Driver (*outside the coach, to Briggs*) The thing is, about these kids, they're like little souls, lost an' wanderin' the cruel heartless streets . . .

The Driver continues his lecture to Briggs outside the coach as the action switches back inside. Colin is at the back seat giving out sweets to Reilly and Co

Reilly How are y' gettin on with Miss, Sir?
Digga We saw y' Sir, goin' into that pub with her.

Further down the aisle Susan is watching and listening as she gives out sweets

Colin (*covering his embarrassment*) Did you?

Reilly Are you in love with her, Sir?
Colin (*making his escape*) All right, you've all got sweets have you?
Reilly (*jeering*) Sir's in love, sir's in love. . . .

Reilly laughs as Colin makes his way back along the aisle

Susan Watch it, Brian!
Reilly (*with feigned innocence*) What, Miss?
Susan You know what.
Reilly Agh hey, he is in love with y' though, isn't he, Miss?
Digga I'll bet he wants to marry y', Miss.
Reilly You'd be better off with me, Miss. I'm better lookin', an'
  I'm sexier. Cool

*Susan gives up playing it straight. She goes up to Reilly and whispers
to him*

Susan (*whispering*) Brian, little boys shouldn't try and act like
  men. The day might come when their words are put to the test!
  (*She walks away*)
Reilly Any day, Miss, any day.
Digga What did she say, what did she say?
Reilly She said she fancied me!

*Briggs and the Driver come on board. Briggs goes to sit opposite
Mrs Kay*

Briggs Well ... We've got a right head-case of a driver.

*The engine comes to life. The Kids cheer. Briggs gives a warning
look, then turns away. As he does so we see a mass of hands raised in
two-fingered gestures to anyone who might be passing. Simul-
taneously the Kids sing*

Song 5: We're Off
Kids (*singing*)   We're off, we're off
                          We're off in a motor car
                          Sixty coppers are after us
                          An' we don't know where we are
                          We turned around a corner
                          Eatin' a Christmas Pie
                          Along came a copper
                          An' he hit me in the eye.
                          I went to tell me mother
                          Me mother wasn't in

I went to tell me Father
An' he kicked me in the bin

Segue into the Travelling Song

Our day out
Our day out
Our day out

which fades to

Our day ...

The following split between all the Kids each taking a different line

Song 6: Look At The Dogs
Look at the dogs
Look at the cats
A broken window in Tesco's
Look at the empty Corpy flats

Look at the streets
Look at the houses
Agh look at that feller
With the hole in the back of his trousers

Look at the pushchairs
Look at the prams
Little kids out shoppin'
With their Mams.

Oh there's our Tracey
There's my mate
He's missed the ~~bloody~~ *Bloomin'* bus
Got up too late

Look at the men
All on the dole
Look at the workers
Layin' cable down that hole

Look at the cars
Look there's a train
Look at the clouds
~~God~~ *Gosh*, I hope it doesn't rain

Segue back into the refrain "Our Day Out", repeated and fading

On the back seat the Little Kid overhears a conversation between Digga and Reilly

Digga Reilly, light up.
Reilly Where's Briggsy?
Digga Up the front. Y' all right, I'll keep the eye out for y'.
Little Kid Agh 'ey, you've got ciggies. I'm gonna tell Miss.
Digga Tell her. She won't do nothin' anyway.
Little Kid I'll tell Sir.
Reilly You do an' I'll gob y'.
Digga Come on, open that window you.
Little Kid Why?
Reilly Why d' y' think? So we can get a bit of fresh air.
Little Kid Well, there is no fresh air round here. You just want to smoke. An' smokin' stunts your growth.
Reilly I'll stunt your growth if y' don't get it open.

Andrews gets up and reaches obligingly for the window

Andrews I'll open it for y' Reilly.

Reilly ducks behind a seat and lights up

Andrews Gis a ciggie. *Clear*
Reilly Sod off. Get y' own ciggies.
Andrews Ah, go on, I opened the window for y'.
Digga Be told you, y' not gettin' no ciggie.

Briggs leaves his seat at the front and heads towards the back of the coach

(*Whispering to Reilly*) Briggs!

Reilly quickly hands the cigarette to Andrews who, unaware of the approaching Briggs seizes it with enthusiasm

Andrews Ooh, thanks Reilly.

Andrews ducks behind the seat and takes a massive drag. He comes up to find Briggs gazing down at him and the ciggie

Briggs Put it out.
Andrews Sir, I wasn't ...
Briggs Put it out lad. Now get to the front of the coach.

Andrews gets up and makes his way to Briggs' seat as Briggs remains at the back

Briggs Was it your ciggie, Reilly?

Reilly Sir, swear on me mother I didn't . . .

Digga Take no notice of him Sir. How can he swear on his mother, she's been dead ten years.

Reilly is about to stick one on Digga

Briggs All right. All right! We don't want any argument. There'll be no smokin' if I stay up here will there?

Briggs takes Andrew's seat. The rest of the coach sing "They've all gone quiet at the back"—one verse to tune "She'll Be Coming Round The Mountain". Mrs Kay and Carol are sitting next to each other, Carol next to the window staring out of it

Carol Isn't it horrible, eh, Miss?

Mrs Kay Mm?

Carol Y' know, all the thingy like; the dirt an' that. (*Pause*) I like them nice places.

Mrs Kay Which places?

Carol Know them places on the telly with gardens, an' trees outside an' that.

Mrs Kay You've got trees in Pilot street haven't you?

Carol They planted some after the riots. But the kids chopped them down an' burnt them on bonfire night. (*Pause*) Miss . . . Miss, y' know when I grow up, Miss, y'know if I work hard an' learn to read an' write, would you think I'd be able to live in one of them nice places?

Mrs Kay (*putting her arm around her*) Well, you could try love, couldn't you eh?

Carol Yeh!

The Kids take up the "Our Day Out" refrain, repeating the line three times. On the back seat Reilly and Digga are stifled by Briggs' presence

Briggs (*suddenly pointing out of the window*) Now, just look at that.

Digga and Reilly glance but see nothing to look at

Digga What?

Briggs (*disgustedly*) What? Can't you see? Look, those buildings, don't you ever observe what's around you?

Reilly It's only the docks, sir.

Briggs You don't get buildings like that anymore. Just look at the
  work that must have gone into that.
Reilly Do you like it down here then, sir?
Briggs I'm often down here at weekends, taking photographs. Are
  you listening, Reilly? There's a wealth of history that won't be
  here much longer.
Reilly My old feller used to work down here.
Briggs What did he think of it?
Reilly He hated it.
Briggs Well, you tell him to take another look and he might
  appreciate it.
Reilly I'll have a job—I haven't seen him for two years. (*He turns
  away and looks out of the window*)

A few seats further down Linda suddenly kneels up on her seat

Linda (*to Jackie*) Ooh, look, there's Sharron. (*She shouts and
  waves*) Sharron . . . Sha . . .
Briggs Linda Croxley!

*Briggs gets up and moves towards Linda. Only at the last moment
does she turn and sit "properly"*

  And what sort of an outfit is that supposed to be for a school
  visit?
Linda (*chewing; contemptuously; staring out of the window*) What?
Briggs Don't you "what" me, young lady.

Linda merely shrugs

  You know very well that on school trips you wear school
  uniform.
Linda Well, Mrs Kay never said nott'n about it.
Briggs You're not talking to Mrs Kay now.
Linda Yeh, I know.
Briggs (*quietly but threateningly*) Now listen here, young lady, I
  don't like your attitude. I don't like it one bit.
Linda What have I said? I haven't said nott'n have I?
Briggs I'm talking about your attitude.

She dismisses him with a glance and turns away

  I'm telling you now, miss. Carry on like this and when we get to
  Conway you'll be spending your time in the coach.
Linda I don't care, I don't wanna see no crappy castle anyway.

Briggs Just count yourself lucky you're not a lad. Now I'm warning. Cause any more unpleasantness on this trip and I shall see to it that it's the last you ever go on. Is that understood? Is it?
Linda (*sighing*) Yeh.
Briggs It better had be.

Briggs makes his way to the front of the coach and addresses the kid next to Andrews

Right, you, what's your name? Wake up.
Maurice Sir, me?
Briggs What's your name?
Maurice McNally, Sir.
Briggs Right, McNally, go and sit at the back.
Maurice Sir, I don't like the back.
Briggs Never mind what you like, go and sit at the back.

Maurice does so

Right, Andrews, shove up.

Briggs sits with Andrews

How long have you been smoking, Andrews?
Andrews Sir, I don't . . . Sir, since I was eight.
Briggs And how old are you now?
Andrews Sir, thirteen, Sir.
Briggs What do your parents say?
Andrews Sir, me mam says nothin' about it but when me dad comes home Sir, Sir, he belts me.
Briggs Because you smoke?
Andrews No Sir, because I won't give him one.

Pause

Briggs Your father works away from home does he?
Andrews What? No, Sir.
Briggs You said, "when he comes home". I thought you meant he was away a lot.
Andrews He is. But he doesn't go to work.
Briggs Well, what does he do then?
Andrews I don't know, Sir, he just comes round every now an' then an' has a barney with me Mam. Then he goes off again. I think he tries to get money off her but she won't give him it though. She hates him. We all hate him.

Briggs Listen, why don't you promise yourself you'll give up smoking? You must realize it's bad for your health.

Andrews Sir, I do, Sir. I've got a terrible cough.

Briggs Then why don't you pack it in?

Andrews Sir, I can't.

Briggs Thirteen and you can't stop smoking?

Andrews No, Sir.

Briggs (*sighing and shaking his head*) Well, you'd better not let me catch you again.

Andrews No, Sir. I won't.

Kids (*variously*) There's the tunnel, the Mersey tunnel, we're goin' through the tunnel.

All the Kids cheer as the bus goes into the tunnel—probably best conveyed by a Black-out

Song 7: The Mersey Tunnel

(*Singing*)   The Mersey tunnel is three miles long
            And the roof is made of glass
            So that you can drive right in
            And watch the ships go past
            There's a plug hole every five yards
            They open it every night
            It lets in all the water and it
            Washes away the sha na na na na na na na na . . .

Briggs rises as they are, he thinks, about to sing an obscenity. He sits down again as he fails to catch them at it

The Kids repeat the verse and Briggs repeats his leap to try and catch them. Again they merely sing 'Sha, na, na, na, etc

They repeat the verse once more. This time Briggs doesn't leap to his feet as the Kids sing:

And washes away the shite!   *Poo*

As Briggs leaps to his feet, too late, the Kids stare from the windows at the "pretty scenery". Briggs glares at them

Girl Sir, are we in Wales yet?

Boy Sir, I need to go to the toilet.

Briggs Yes, well you should have thought of that before you got on the coach, shouldn't you?

Boy Sir, I did, Sir, I've got a weak bladder.

Briggs Then a little control will help to strengthen it.
Maurice Sir, Sir, I'm wettin' meself.
Digga Are we stoppin' for toilets, Sir?

All the Kids take up the cry in one form or another. Groans, moans and cries of "toilet". "I wanna go the toilet"

Briggs For God's sake. Just shut up, all of you shut up!
Mrs Kay Mr B——
Briggs I said shut up. (*Then he realizes*) Erm, sorry, sorry. Mrs Kay?
Mrs Kay I would like to go to the toilet myself!

Briggs stares at her

Milton (*raising his hand*) Sir . . . Sir . . .
Briggs (*snapping*) Yes, Milton.
Milton Sir, I wondered if you were aware that over six hundred people per year die from ruptured bladders.
Briggs (*conceding defeat; turning to the Driver*) Pull in at the toilets up ahead, will you? (*Turning to the Kids*) Right, I want everybody back on this coach in two minutes. Those who need the toilets, off you go.

Most of the Kids get off the coach and go off as if to the toilets

Reilly, Digga and a small group form some yards away from the coach, obviously smoking

Colin (*approaching them*) All right, lads. Shouldn't be too long before we're in Wales.
Little Kid Wales, that's in the country isn't it, Sir?
Colin A lot of it's countryside, yes, but. . . .
Reilly Lots of woods eh, Sir?
Colin Well, woods, yes mountains and lakes.
Reilly An' you're gonna show Miss the woods are y', Sir?
Colin Just watch it Brian, right?
Reilly Ah, I only meant was y' gonna show her the plants an' the trees.
Colin I know quite well what you meant. (*He turns to go*) And if I was you I'd put that fag out before you burn your hand. If Mr Briggs catches you you'll spend the rest of the day down at the front of the coach with him and you don't want that to happen do you? Now come on, put it out.

Reilly puts out the cigarette and Colin walks away

Reilly (*shouting after him*) I'll show Miss the woods for y', Sir.

Throughout the above all the other Kids have made their way back on to the coach

Mrs Kay (*as she returns*) Come on, Brian, come on. (*She ushers them on board*) OK, Ronnie, I think that's the lot.

The bus starts

Little Kid Miss, miss.
Mrs Kay Yes.
Little Kid Miss, I wanna go the toilet.
Kids Aah, shurrup.
Driver Get ready, a humpety backed bridge. . . .

As they go over the bridge all the passengers are bumped off their seats

Two Bored Girls It's borin'
        (*in unison*)   It's bleedin' borin.
                Another minute here an' I'll be snorin'.
                Lookin' at loads of roads, Miss
                When are we gonna stop?
                There's nothin' to do
                Only look at the view
                An' if you've seen one hill
                You've seen the bleedin' lot.
                God! It's borin', isn't it borin',
                It's borin,
                It's bleedin' borin'.

The other Kids take up, quietly, the refrain of "It's Borin', It's Bleedin' Borin'". At the front of the coach Mrs Kay is having a word with Ronnie

Mrs Kay Ronnie, I was wondering if there was somewhere we could stop for a little while, have a cup of tea and let them stretch their legs?
Driver All right, Mrs Kay, there's a cafe just up ahead; d' y' want me to pull in?
Mrs Kay Thanks, Ron.

Song 8 begins as the Kids dismantle the coach and re-set the seats to form the cafe/shop and picnic area. (**Note:** *If doubling is necessary the actress playing Susan changes here to play cafe/shop proprietress*)

Song 8: Straight Line

Briggs (*singing*)	All right! Let's get this straight.
	We're only stopping for a quarter of an hour
	When you leave the bus you will get in line and wait
	We do not want this visit turning sour.
Mrs Kay (*singing*)	It's all right everybody there will still be lots of time
	For you to stretch your legs and let off steam
	You're free to leave the bus now but please don't go getting lost.
	The shop's that way, for those who want ice cream.

The Kids cheer as they set up the shop/cafe

Briggs	All right! Now that's enough
	You're behaving like a gang of common scruffs.
Mrs Kay	By the book, Mr Briggs?
Briggs	Yes, why not by the book?
	I want them looking tidy
Mrs Kay	That's one thing they'll never look.
Briggs	Come on now get in line, I said line up, do what you're told.
Mrs Kay	For a straight line is a wonderful thing to behold.

The music continues as underscoring as Briggs addresses the Kids

Briggs Now the people who run these places provide a good and valuable service to travellers like ourselves and so I want to see this place treated with the sort of respect it deserves. Now come on, let's have a straight line, in twos.

Mrs Kay is at the front of the queue which is being formed. Inevitably there are kids who don't conform exactly to Briggs's concept of a straight line

Come on you two, get in line. You two! Reilly, get in line, lad. I
said in line . . .

Mrs Kay Mr Briggs . . .

Briggs I think it's under control Mrs Kay, thank you. (*Barking at the Kids*) Come on! Cut out the fidgeting. Just stand. Straight! That's more . . . RONSON. Come here, lad.

Mrs Kay Mr Briggs. . . .

Briggs It's all right Mrs Kay! (*To Ronson*) Now just where do you think you are, lad?

Ronson (*a beat as he wonders*) Sir. . . . Sir, Wales?

Briggs (*almost screaming by now*) Get in line, lad.

(*Singing*)	All right. That's looking fine.
	Chaos turned to order in a stroke.
Mrs Kay	Quite amazing, Mr Briggs, they're standing in a line!
Briggs	And it's important, Mrs Kay, it's not a joke.
Mrs Kay	Oh yes, of course it's awfully serious, I'm terribly impressed
	Such achievements are the hallmark of the great
	A quite remarkable example of a very straight, straight line
	Congratulations, Mr Briggs it's . . . well it's straight!
Briggs	I think that's good, don't you?
Mrs Kay	They do so well at standing two by two.
Briggs	They do us credit, Mrs Kay.
Mrs Kay	Perhaps that's true,
	If you stake your reputation on a stationary queue!
Briggs	Come on, it's better than a rabble, there they are as good as gold,
Mrs Kay	Oh, a straight line is a wonderful thing to behold.

Briggs (*speaking*) With organization, Mrs Kay, with organization
it can be done.

Mrs Kay, the other Teachers and the Kids hit the song finale as per Hollywood, splitting into two lines, hands waving and legs kicking

All (*singing*)	A straight line is a wonderful thing to behold!

On the last note they are back in twos, lined up

Shopkeeper Right, two at a time.

The Kids charge as one into the shop

Briggs (*apoplectic*) Stop, I said stop … stop …

Mrs Kay takes his arm and diverts him

Mrs Kay Oh, let's forget about them for a while. Come and have some coffee out of my flask. Come on.

A sea of Kids in front of a sweet counter and a harrassed Shopkeeper

Shopkeeper Fifty-four, the chocolate bars are fifty-four.
Maurice That's robbery.
Kid They're only thirty pence down our way.
Girl 2 Yeh, an' they're twice the size.
Kid Ey, missis, give us one of them up there.

As the Shopkeeper turns her back the Kids begin robbing sweets

Shopkeeper Hey. Put that down, give that here. Where're your teachers? They should be in here with you.
Kid What for? They couldn't afford to buy anything, the prices you charge.
Shopkeeper There's a surcharge for school parties and if you don't like it you can get out.

There is a Black-out on the shop area and the action is frozen as we see Briggs and Mrs Kay outside, Briggs reluctant, keeping an eye on the shop

Mrs Kay Isn't it nice to get away from them for a few minutes.
Briggs To be quite honest, Mrs Kay, I think we should be in there, looking after them.

There is a Black-out on the teachers and the action is frozen as the Lights come up on the shop area

Shopkeeper (*amidst the chaos*) 'Ere. Put that down. Keep your hands to yourselves.
Girl 1 How much are the Bountys?

The Shopkeeper turns her back and much of the counter contents go into the Kids' pockets

Shopkeeper Now, just a minute, give me that hand. Come on, put it back.

Kid Y' big robber.

Girl 1 Ey you, I haven't robbed nottn'.

Milton How much are the penny chews?

Shopkeeper Tenpence, the penny chews are tenpence. (*She clouts a kid*) Take your 'ands off!

Milton But they're called "penny" chews.

Shopkeeper Yes! They're called penny chews but they cost tenpence each.

Maurice It's robbery that.

Milton If the penny chews cost tenpence each don't you think they should be called tenpenny chews?

Shopkeeper But they're not called tenpenny chews. They're called penny chews and they cost tenpence! Right?

Milton I hope you realize this represents a serious breach of the Trades Descriptions Act.

Shopkeeper And I hope you realize that if you don't shut up there'll be a serious breach of your bloody head!

Ronson D' y' sell chips?

Shopkeeper NO!

There is a Black-out in the shop area and the action is frozen. Lights up on Mrs Kay and Briggs outside the café

Briggs There's not just our school to think of you know. What about those who come after us? They're dependent on the goodwill of the people who run these places.

Mrs Kay Considering the profit they make from the kids I don't think they've got too much to complain about.

The Kids begin to emerge from the shop/café area moaning about prices and dismissing the place

Mr Briggs. I didn't ask you to come on this trip.

Briggs No, but the headmaster did.

Throughout the following song the coach is re-assembled. By the end of the song everyone is sitting in his or her seat and the coach is on its way again

Song 9: Penny Chews
Kids (*singing*)   Penny chews are tenpence in this caff
                        Yes penny chews are tenpence in this caff

They say prices are inflated
But it's robbery, let's face it
When penny chews are tenpence, what a laugh.

They're chargin' stupid prices for their sweets
Yes they're chargin' stupid prices for their
    sweets
An' they must be makin' quids
Out of all poor starvin' kids
Cause they're chargin' stupid prices for their
    sweets

No they shouldn't be allowed to charge that
    much
They shouldn't be allowed to charge that much
It's robbery it's last it's
Just a bunch of thievin' bastards
Who think that everyone they meet's an easy
    touch.

Well it would have cost us more than we have
    got
Yes it would have cost us more than we have got
Who swindle an' defraud it
When they know we can't afford it
It's a good job that we robbed the bleedin' lot!

*Colin, who has been sitting with Briggs, gets up to check that
everything is all right. As he gets near Linda's seat her mate, Jackie,
taps her on the shoulder and points him out. Linda turns and smiles
at Colin*

Linda Sir, are y' comin' to sit by me, are y'?

Jackie Don't sit by her, Sir, come an' sit by me.

Colin I've got my seat down at the front, thanks Jackie.

Linda Here, Sir.

Colin What, Linda?

Linda Come here, I wanna tell y' somethin'.

Colin Well, go on.

Linda Ah hey, Sir. I don't want everyone to hear. Come on, just
sit here while I tell y'.

Jackie Go on, Sir, she won't bite y'.

Linda Come on.

Colin reluctantly sits. Jackie's head is poked through the space between the seats

Colin Well? What is it?

Linda and Jackie laugh

You're not going to tell me a joke are you?

They laugh again

Look, Linda, I'll have to go I've ...

Linda quickly links her arm through Colin's and holds him there

Linda No, Sir, listen, listen. She said I wouldn't tell y', but I will. Sir, Sir, I think you're lovely.

Colin (*quickly getting up*) Linda! (*He returns to his seat next to Briggs*)

Linda I told him. I said I would. Oh God, he's boss him, isn't he, eh?

Jackie Oh, go way, you. You've got no chance. He's goin' with Miss.

Linda He might chuck her. Might start goin' with me. Might marry me.

Jackie (*shrieking*) Oh, don't be mental. You'll never get a husband like Sir. You'll end up marryin' someone like your old feller.

Linda You're just jealous, girl.

Jackie Get lost.

Linda turns and dismisses her, stares out of the window and begins to sing

Song 10: I'm In Love With Sir

Linda (*singing*)   I'm in love with Sir
But Sir doesn't care
Cos Sir's in love with her
Over there
With the hair
It isn't fair

She turns to Jackie

If I was the wife of a man like Sir
My life would not be full of trouble and care

I'd look forward to the nights and we'd make
        a perfect pair
Me and Sir

I'm in love with Sir
But Sir doesn't care
Cos Sir's in love with her
Over there
With the hair
It isn't fair

If I could marry Sir I'd be right
I wouldn't need to work and we would stay in
        every night
We'd have some lovely holidays and I would
        wash his collars
Really white

The Kids   She's in love with Sir
But Sir doesn't care
Cos Sir's in love with her
Over there
With the hair
It isn't fair

Jackie   You'll be the wife of a man like your dad
He'll disappear when you grow fat
You'll be left with the kids and you'll live in a
Council flat

The Kids   She's in love with Sir
But Sir doesn't care
Cos Sir's in love with her
Over there
With the hair
It isn't fair

Linda   I'm in love with Sir.

Mrs Kay has been talking to the Driver. She returns to her seat next to Carol

Briggs (*to Colin next to him*) You know what Mrs Kay's problem is don't you?
Colin (*trying to keep out of it*) Mm?

Briggs Well! She thinks I can't see through all this woolly-minded liberalism. You know what I mean? All right.

Girls One and Two, Little Kid and Maurice are arguing about sweets. Briggs machine guns a "be quiet" at them

I mean she has her methods and I have mine but this setting herself up as the champion of the non-academics! I mean, it might look like love and kindness but it doesn't fool me. And it doesn't do kids a scrap of good. I think you've got to risk being disliked if you're going to do anything for kids like these. They've got enough freedom at home haven't they? Eh? With their five quid pocket money and telly till all hours, video games and that. Eh? I don't know about you, I don't know about you but to me her philosophy's all over the place. (*Pause*) Eh?

Colin (*reluctant, but having to answer*) Actually I don't think it's got anything to do with a formulated philosophy.

Briggs You mean you've not noticed all this anti-establishment, just-let-the-kids-roam-wild, don't check 'em sort of attitude?

Colin Of course I've noticed. But she's like this all the time. This trip isn't organized on the basis of any profound theory.

Briggs Well, what's the method she does work to, then? Mm? Eh? I mean, you know her better than me, go on you tell me.

Colin Well, she, for one thing, she likes them.

Briggs Who?

Colin The kids. She likes kids.

Briggs What's that got to do with it?

Pause

Colin The principle behind this trip is that the kids should have a good day out.

Briggs And isn't that what I'm saying? But if they're going to have a good and stimulating day it's got to be better planned and executed than this.

Briggs suddenly notices that the coach has turned off the expected route

What's this? Where are we going? This isn't ...

Mrs Kay Oh, it's all right, Mr Briggs. I've checked with the driver, we thought it might be a good idea if we called in at the zoo for an hour. We've got plenty of time.

Briggs But, but this trip was arranged so that we could visit Conway Castle.

Mrs Kay Ooh, we're going there as well. I know you're very fond of ruins. Now listen everyone, as an extra bonus, we've decided to call in here at the zoo.

There are cheers all round

Briggs But look, we can't . . .

Mrs Kay Now the rest of the staff will be around if you want to know anything about the various animals, although it's not much good asking me because I don't know one monkey from the next . . .

Briggs Mrs Kay . . .

Mrs Kay (*ignoring Briggs*) But, Progress Class, we're very lucky today to have Mr Briggs with us because Mr Briggs is something of an expert in natural history. He's something of a David Bellamy, aren't you Mr Briggs? So if you want to know more about the animals, ask Mr Briggs. Now come on. Leave your things on the coach.

The underscoring for Song 11 begins as the teachers set up the zoo and café

The Kids spread out in groups around the auditorium as though at different parts of the zoo

Song 11: Zoo Song (Who's Watching Who?)

Kids (*singing as they move*)
Sealions and penguins

Drums

Swimming in the zoo

Drums

What do seals eat?

Drums

Pilchard sarnies
Who's watching who's watching who's watching who?
Who's watching who's watching who's watching who?

Centipedes and pythons
Wriggling at the zoo
What do snakes eat?
Wrigley's spearmint
Who's watching who's watching who's watching
   who?
Who's watching who's watching who's watching
   who?

Middle eight

Elephants from Africa, an Aussie kangaroo
All flown in on jumbo jets and stuck here in the
   zoo

The two Bored Girls speak, with drums underscoring their verse

Bored Girls   It's borin'
It's bleedin' borin'
The lions are all asleep
They're not even roarin'.
It's just a load of parrots
Bleedin' monkeys an' giraffes,
It isn't worth a carrot
I come here for a laugh

But it's borin'
It's really borin'
We shoulda stayed at school
An' done some drawin'
A zoo's just stupid animals
An' some of them are smelly
I think zoo's are better
When y' watch them on the telly.
It's borin'
Bleedin' borin' . . .

As they close their verse the other Kids take up the song again

Coloured birds in cages
Do you want to fly away
What do birds eat?
Sir, Bird's custard.
Who's watching who's watching etc.

Briggs and a group of Kids enter and look down into the bear pit

Briggs And a brown bear is an extremely dangerous animal. You see those claws, they could leave a really nasty mark.

Andrews Could it kill y', Sir?

Briggs Well why do you think they keep it in a pit?

Ronson I think that's cruel, sir. Don't you?

Briggs Not if it's treated well, no. Don't forget, Ronson, that an animal like this would have been born into captivity. It's always had walls around it so it won't know anything other than this sort of existence, will it?

Ronson I'll bet it does.

Girl 1 How do you know? Sir's just told you hasn't he? If it was born in a cage an' it's lived all its life in a cage well it won't know any different will it? So it won't want anything different.

Ronson Well, why does it kill people then?

Andrews What's that got to do with it, dick head?

Ronson It kills people because people are cruel to it. They keep it in here, in this pit so when it gets out it's bound to go mad an' want to kill people. Can't y' see?

Andrews Sir, he's thick. Tell him to shutup.

Ronson I'm not thick. Even if it has lived all its life in there it must know musn't it, Sir?

Briggs Know what, Ronson?

Ronson Know about other ways of livin'. About bein' free. Sir it only kills people cos they keep it trapped in here but if it was free an' it was treated all right it'd start to be friends with y' then wouldn't it? If y' were doin' nothing wrong to it it wouldn't want to kill y'.

Briggs Well, I wouldn't be absolutely sure about that, Ronson.

Andrews Sir's right. Bears kill y' cos it's in them to kill y'.

Girl 2 Ah, come on, Sir, let's go to the Pets Corner.

Andrews No way, Sir, let's see the big ones.

Briggs We'll get round them all eventually.

Girl 2 Come on then, Sir, let's go the Pets Corner . . .

Girl 1 and Girl 2 go to link arms with Briggs. He shrugs them off

Briggs Now walk properly, properly . . .

Girl 2 Agh hey, Sir, all the other teachers let y' link them.

Mrs Kay enters with another group of Kids. She has got Kids on either side, linking her arms

Mrs Kay How are you getting on? Plying you with questions?

Briggs Yes, yes, they've been—very good.

Mrs Kay I'm just going for a cup of coffee. Want to join me?

Briggs Well, I was just on my way to the Pets Corner ...

Andrews It's all right, Sir, we'll go on our own.

Mrs Kay Oh come on, they'll be all right.

Briggs But can these people be trusted, Mrs Kay?

Mrs Kay They'll be all right. Colin and Susan are walking round. And the place is walled in.

Andrews Go on, Sir, you go an' have a cuppa. You can trust us.

Briggs Ah, can I though? If I go off for a cup of tea with Mrs Kay, can you people be trusted to act responsibly?

Kids Yes Sir.

Jimmy Sir, what sort of a bird's that, Sir?

Briggs Erm. Oh, let me see, yes it's a macaw.

Mrs Kay Come on.

Briggs (*following Mrs Kay*) They're very good talkers.

Mrs Kay and Briggs move to the café area

Kevin I told y' it wasn't a parrot.

Jimmy (*trying to get the bird to talk*) Liverpool, Liverpool. Come on say it, y' dislocated sparrow.

Kids   Mountain lions and panthers
(singing)   Leopards in the zoo
                  What do lions eat?

Jimmy ⎫
Kevin ⎭ (*together*) Evertonians

Kids   Who's watching who's watching, who's watching who?

                       Who's watching who's watching who's watching who

Mrs Kay and Briggs are sitting in the café area, two teas and a couple of cakes in front of them. The Kids are looking through the "windows" of the café

Kids   Teachers in the café
                       Takin' tea for two
                       What do they eat
(*Speaking*) Ooh, chocolate cream cakes!

Briggs and Mrs Kay suddenly notice hungry eyes on their cakes

Mrs Kay (*waving them away*) Ooh go on, go away ... shoo ...

The Kids disperse and go off singing

Kids   Who's watching who's watching who's watching
                       who
                       Who's watching who's watching who's watching
                       who?

Briggs Another tea, Mrs Kay?

Mrs Kay Oh, call me Helen. Do you know I loathe being called
Mrs Kay. Do you know I tried to get the kids to call me by my
first name. I told them, call me Helen, not Mrs Kay. They were
outraged. They wouldn't do it. So it's good old Mrs Kay again.
Oh, no, no more tea thanks.

Briggs They're really quite interested, the kids, aren't they?

Mrs Kay In the animals, oh yes. And it's such a help having you
here because you know so much about this sort of thing.

Briggs Well, I wouldn't say I was an expert but ... you know,
perhaps when we're back at school I could come along to your
department and show some slides I've got.

Mrs Kay Would you really? Oh, Mr Briggs, we'd love that.

Briggs Well, look, I'll sort out which free periods I've got and
we'll organize it for then.

*Colin and Susan approach the café area. The Kids quickly line up in
the sort of orderly queue Briggs would approve of*

Susan Ready when you are.

Mrs Kay Are they all back?

Susan It's amazing, we came around the corner and they're all
there, lined up waiting to get on the bus.

Mrs Kay Wonders will never cease.

Briggs OK. (*Seeing the Kids*) Well, look at this, Mrs Kay, they're
learning at last eh? Right, all checked and present? On board
then. ...

*The Kids go to climb aboard the bus just as an animal keeper, all
polo-neck and wellies, rushes towards them*

Keeper Hold it right there.

Mrs Kay Hello, have we forgotten something?

Keeper Are you supposed to be in charge of this lot?

Mrs Kay Why, what's the matter?

Keeper Children? They're not bloody children, they're animals.
It's not the zoo back there, this is the bloody zoo, here.

Briggs Excuse me! Would you mind controlling your language and telling me what's going on?

The Keeper ignores Briggs, pushes past him and confronts the Kids

Keeper Right. Where are they?

Innocent faces and replies of "what", "where's what?"

You know bloody well what ...

Briggs (*intercepting the Keeper*) Now look, this has just gone far enough. Would you ...

He is interrupted by the loud clucking of a hen. The Keeper strides up to a Kid and pulls open his jacket. A bantam hen is revealed

Keeper (*taking the hen; addressing the other kids*) Right, now I want the rest.

There is a moment's hesitation before the flood gates are opened. Animals appear from every conceivable hiding place. Briggs glares as the animals are rounded up. The Kids stay in place, waiting for the thunder

Briggs I trusted you lot. And this is the way you repay me. (*A pause as he fights to control his anger*) I trusted all of you but it's obvious that trust is something you know nothing about.

Ronson Sir, we only borrowed them.

Briggs (*screaming*) Shut up, lad! Is it any wonder that people won't do anything for you? The moment we start to treat you like real people, what happens? Well, that man was right. You act like animals, animals.

Mrs Kay Come on now, take the animals back.

The Kids are relieved at finding a way to go. As they move off Briggs remains

Briggs And that's why you're treated like animals, why you'll always be treated like animals.

Kids sing very quietly as they exit

Kids (*singing*)   Our day out
                                  Our day out
Briggs (*alone*) ANIMALS!

There is a Black-out

END OF ACT ONE

ACT II

The Teachers and the Kids are outside Conway Castle

Briggs We'll split into four groups Mrs Kay. Each member of staff will be responsible for one group. It will take approximately one and a quarter hours to tour the castle and at three fifteen we will re-assemble at the coach. Walk round in twos, and I mean walk! Right, my group, this way ...

The party divides into groups. The Kids in Briggs's group follow him with little enthusiasm

(*pointing up at the castle walls*) Now, those large square holes just below the battlements; long planks of wood were supported there and that's where the archers would fire from if the castle was under attack. Something really interesting up there. If you look at that tower you'll see that it's not quite perpendicular. What does perpendicular mean?

Maurice I don't know.

Milton Sir, Sir ...

Briggs Yes?

Milton Sir, straight up.

Sniggers from the other Kids

Briggs Are you listening, lad? You might just learn something.

Song 12: Castle Song

(*Singing*)
I find it so depressing
I just can't understand
Your failure to appreciate
A thing so fine and grand
Your heritage, your history
You can touch it with your hand
The Yanks have nothing like it

Milton Sir, but they've got Disneyland.

Briggs (*speaking*) Disneyland!

(*Singing*)
That's not the same at all, this is history, this is real

	It should make you feel so proud, so
	thrilled, so awed
	Just standing here for centuries, how
	does that make you feel?
	Come on, speak up, don't mumble lad.
Kids	Sir, it makes us feel dead bored.

The music continues as underscoring

Briggs Bored! Yes and you'll be bored forever; do you want to know why? Because you put nothing in. You invest in nothing. And if you invest in nothing you get nothing in return. This way. Come on, quickly, move.

As Briggs leads his group off, Reilly and Digga slip away from it and get the ciggies out. They hide when they hear Colin approaching. Linda and Jackie are with him

Colin (*singing*)	Now though these walls are very thick
	In places fifteen feet
	Just think how cold it must have been
	With no real form of heat
	Even in the summertime
	It must have been quite cold
Linda	I wonder how they managed, Sir,
	To keep warm in days of old.
Jackie ⎫ (*together*) **Linda** ⎭	Tell us, Sir go on,
	Tell us everything you know
	We want to learn from you, Sir
	Yes we do, Ooh Ooh
	We really think you're great, Sir
	Tell us everything you know
	We'd be really brainy, Sir,
	If all the teachers were like you.

Colin Well. They'd obviously ... Where's everybody else gone? Where are the others?

Jackie Sir, they kept droppin' out as you were talkin'.

Colin Oh, God!

Linda Oh it's all right, Sir, we're dead interested. Y' can keep showin' us around.

Colin (*sighing*) All right, what was I saying?

Linda You were tellin' us how they kept warm in the olden days.

Colin Well for one thing ... Linda.

(*Singing*)	They wore much thicker clothing
Linda	Even damsels in distress?
Colin	I expect they *all* had more sense
	Than to walk around half dressed.
Linda ⎫ (*together*)	We seen this movie once, Sir,
Jackie ⎭	Where they had some better ways
	To keep each other cosy, Sir,
	Back in them olden days.

Colin (*speaking*) All right, Linda, all right . . .

Linda ⎫ (*together*)	Tell us, Sir, go on
Jackie ⎭	Tell us everything you know
	We want to learn from you, Sir
	Yes we do, Ooh Ooh.
	We really think you're great, Sir
	Tell us everything you know
	We'd be really brainy, Sir,
	If all the teachers were like you.

Linda Sir, it's dead spooky here. Sir, I think it's haunted. (*She grabs his arm*)

Colin Don't be silly.

Linda (*throwing her arms around him*) I'm frightened.

Colin Don't do that, Linda.

Linda But I'm frightened. (*She holds him tightly*)

Jackie (*also grabbing him*) Sir, so am I.

Colin (*freeing himself*) Now, girls, stop being silly. Stop it!

(*Singing*)	There's nothing to be frightened of
	There's no such things as ghosts
	Just look how this position
	Gives a clear view of the coast
Girls	But we'd rather look at you, Sir
Colin	Yes, but girls, you're here to learn
Girls	Oh Sir, you're so impressive when
	You behave so strong and firm
	Tell us, Sir, go on
	Then we won't be scared at all
	We feel so warm and safe when we're
	with you Ooh Ooh
	We know you will protect us, Sir
	Cos you're all strong and tall
	And if we can't believe in ghosts
	We can still believe in you.

Digga and Reilly lean out unnoticed from their hiding position. They touch the girls who scream and grab Colin again

Linda It touched me.
Colin What did?
Linda Oh, it did.

Reilly and Digga jeer and run off

Colin God. Come on, girls, come on.

They follow Colin off

Carol is sitting on the battlements, looking out over the estuary. Nearby, on a bench, Mrs Kay is sitting back enjoying the sun

Mrs Kay Why don't you go and have a look around the castle Carol? You haven't seen it yet.
Carol Miss, I don't like it. It's horrible. I'd rather sit here with you an' look at the lake.
Mrs Kay That's the sea.
Carol Yeh, that's what I mean.

Andrews runs on and joins Carol and Mrs Kay

Andrews Miss, Miss, I just thought of this great idea; Miss wouldn't it be smart if we had somethin' like this castle round our way. The kids wouldn't get into trouble, would they, if they had somewhere like this to play.
Carol Miss, we couldn't have somethin' like this round our way, could we?
Mrs Kay Why not?
Carol 'Cos if we had somethin' like this we'd only wreck it wouldn't we?
Andrews No, we wouldn't.
Carol We would. That's why we never have nothin' nice round our way—we'd smash it up. The Corporation knows that an' so why should they waste their time and money. They'd give us nice things if we looked after them, but we don't do we?
Andrews Miss, d' y' know what I think about it, Miss?
Mrs Kay Go on, John, what?
Andrews Miss, Miss, if all this belonged to us—like it wasn't the Corporation's but it was something that we owned, well we wouldn't let no-one wreck it would we? Eh? We'd look after it wouldn't we? Defend it. D' y' know what I mean, Miss?

Mrs Kay Yes, I think I do.

Briggs enters

What you're saying . . .

Briggs Right. You two, off. Go on move.

Carol Sir, where?

Briggs Anywhere girl. Just move. I want to talk to Mrs Kay. Well, come on then.

The two Kids reluctantly wander off, Briggs waiting until they are out of hearing

Mrs Kay (*quietly angry*) I was talking to those children.

Briggs Yes, an' I'm talking to you, Mrs Kay. This has got to stop.

Mrs Kay Pardon me. What's got to stop?

Briggs What! Can't you see what's going on? It's a shambles, the whole ill-organized affair. Just look what they did at the zoo. Look.

A group of Kids run past playing chase and tick

They're just left to race and chase and play havoc. God knows what the castle authorities must think. Now look, when you bring children like this into this sort of environment you can't afford to just let them roam free.

Kids rush past

They're just like town dogs let off the leash in the country. My God, for some of them it's the first time they've been farther than Birkenhead.

Mrs Kay (*quietly*) I know. And I was just thinking; it's a shame really isn't it? We bring them out to a crumbling pile of bricks and mortar and they think they're in the fields of heaven.

Briggs You *are* on their side aren't you?

Mrs Kay Absolutely, Mr Briggs, absolutely.

A couple of kids shout to try and hear the echo of their names

Briggs Look, all I want to know from you is what you're going to do about this chaos?

Mrs Kay Well I'd suggest that if you want the chaos to stop you should simply look at it not as chaos but what it actually is— kids, with a bit of space around them, making a bit of noise. All right, so the Head asked you to come along—but can't you just relax? There's no point in pretending that a day out to Wales is going to be of some great educational benefit to them. It's too late for them. Most of these kids were rejects the day they came into the world. We're not going to solve anything today, Mr Briggs. Can't we just give them a good day out? Mm? At least we could try and do that.

Briggs Well that's a fine attitude isn't it? That's a fine attitude for a member of the teaching profession.

Mrs Kay (*beginning to let her temper go*) Well, what's your alternative? Eh? Pretending? Pretending that they've got some sort of a future ahead of them,? Even if you cared for these kids you couldn't help to make a future for them. You won't educate them because nobody wants them educated.

Briggs Listen, Mrs Kay . . .

Mrs Kay No, you listen, Mr Briggs, you listen and perhaps you'll stop fooling yourself. Teach them? Teach them what? You'll never teach them because nobody knows what to do with them. Ten years ago you could teach them to stand in a line, you could teach them to obey, to expect little more than a lousy factory job. But now they haven't even got that to aim for. Mr Briggs, you won't teach them because you're in a job that's designed and funded to fail! There's nothing for them to do, any of them; most of them were born for factory fodder, but the factories have closed down.

Briggs And I suppose that's the sort of stuff you've been pumping into their minds.

Mrs Kay (*laughing*) And you really think they'd understand?

Briggs I'm not going to spend any more time arguing with you. You may have organized this visit, but I'm the one who was sent by the headmaster to supervise. Now, either you take control of the children in your charge or I'll be forced to abandon this visit and order everyone home.

Mrs Kay Well, that's your decision. But I'm not going to let you prevent the kids from having some fun. If you want to abandon this visit, you'd better start walking because we're not going home. We're going down to the beach! (*She walks away from Briggs*) Colin, round everybody up. Come on everybody, we're going to the beach.

Briggs The beach?

The Kids and other Teachers enter as the introduction to the Beach Song is played

Mrs Kay You can't come all the way to the seaside and not pay a
 visit to the beach.

*The Kids sing (to the tune of the Mersey Tunnel song) as they set up
the rocks and the beach*

Song 12a: Beach Song

Kids   The castle's just a load of stones
                      It's borin' and it's dead
                      Can't even fire the cannons
                      Cos they're blocked off at the end
                      So we're goin' to the seashore
                      An' Miss says we can
                      Build a better castle there
                      With just the bloody sand

*Continue underscoring as the Kids begin to whip off their shoes and
socks, Mrs Kay doing the same. The bored girls firmly keeping their
shoes and socks on*

Bored Girls   It's borin'
                      It's bleedin' borin'
                      It's only a load of sand
                      An' seagulls squawkin'
Bored 1   God, we've been here bloody hours
                      Can't we go home yet?
Bored 2   Look at the water
Bored 1   Water's borin'
                      All it does is make y' wet
Both   Yeh it's borin'
                      Really borin'.
Kids   We're gonna find some thingies
                      In the pools and in the rocks
                      We're gonna shout an' run about
                      Without our shoes and socks

*They run about until almost as one the immensity of the place hits
them. They each stand, transfixed, looking out to sea and squelching
their toes in the wet sand*

The music becomes slow and wave-like

                      The sea's gi-bleedin'-gantic
                      It must be really wide

> Cos we can't even see
> What's over on the other side

The sound of the ocean is heard

The Driver runs on with a ball

Driver Mrs Kay, all right if I take some of them off for a game of footie?
Mrs Kay Yes.

Some of the Kids run off with the Driver

Carol (*tugging at Mrs Kay's sleeve*) Miss, when do we have to go home?
Mrs Kay What's the matter, love? Aren't you enjoying yourself?
Carol Yeh. But I don't wanna go home. I wanna stay here.
Mrs Kay Carol love, we're here for at least another hour yet. Now why don't you start enjoying yourself instead of worrying about going home.
Carol Cos I don't wanna go home.
Mrs Kay Carol love, we have to go home in the end. This is a special day. it can't be like this all the time.
Carol Why not?

Mrs Kay looks at Carol, sighs and puts her arm around her

Mrs Kay I don't know love. Come on, let's go and play football with the others.
Carol Nah. (*She breaks away and wanders off*)

Mrs Kay watches her for a moment and then turns to the two bored girls

Mrs Kay Come on, you two; let's go and play football.
Bored 1 Miss, what for?
Mrs Kay What for? Oh, you don't like football. (*Suddenly mimicking them*) Football's borin', it's dead borin', it's borin', borin', borin'.

They look at her as though she's lost a screw

Bored 1 We like football.
Mrs Kay Well, come on then. (*She begins to go*) Come on.
Bored 2 Miss, where?
Mrs Kay (*almost screaming*) To play football, you said you liked football. Well?

Bored 1 We do on the telly!

Bored 2 Don't like playin' it though. Playin' football's dead——

Mrs Kay, hands outstretched to throttle them both, rushes at them

The two girls suddenly move and are chased off by Mrs Kay

Colin, Susan, Linda, Jackie and other girls are examining the rock pools. Reilly, Digga and a small group of followers are having a smoke behind some large rocks. Reilly comes out from behind the rocks and shouts over to Susan

Reilly All right, Miss?

Colin (*quietly*) Here we go.

Andrews (*to Reilly*) Gis a drag.

Digga Buy your own.

Andrews Don't be a rat. Come on.

Reilly holds out the butt, Andrews goes to take it but before he can, Reilly drops it into the sand and treads on it

Reilly (*shouting across*) Y' comin' for a walk with me, Miss?

Colin (*standing and shouting back*) Look I'm warning you, Reilly . . .

Susan Leave it.

Colin I'm just about sick of him.

Susan Well, go over and have a word with him.

Colin I've tried that but whatever I do I can't seem to get through to friend Brian.

Susan I wonder if I could.

Reilly (*shouting over*) What are y' scared of, Miss?

Susan (*to Colin*) You go back with the others.

Colin What are you going to——

Susan Go on.

Colin and the group of girls begin to move away

Linda Is Miss gonna sort him out, Sir?

Jackie He needs sortin' out doesn't he, Sir?

Linda He's all right really y' know, Sir. He's great when y' get him on his own.

Jackie Oh! An' how do you know?

Linda I just do.

Colin and the girls exit

Susan begins to walk towards Reilly, slow and determined, staring straight at him, provocatively. Reilly's smile begins to disappear and he gulps for air. Susan steps straight up to him, and pins him against the rocks

Susan (*huskily*) Well, Brian. I'm here.

Reilly 'Ey, Miss.

Susan I'm all yours ... handsome ... sexy ... Brian!

Reilly Don't mess, Miss.

Susan (*putting her arms around him*) I'm not messing, Big Boy. I'm very, very serious.

Briggs suddenly enters, sees what he thinks is happening, turns and exits again

Susan carries on, unaware of Briggs' entrance

Susan What's wrong?

Reilly I was only havin' a laugh, Miss.

Susan You mean—don't tell me you weren't being serious Brian.

Reilly I was only jokin' with y', Miss.

Susan (*dropping the act*) Now you listen to me, Brian Reilly, you're a handsome lad, but I suggest that in future you stay in your own league, instead of trying to take on ladies who could break you into little pieces. All right? We'll leave it at that shall we?

Reilly Yes, Miss.

Susan smiles at Reilly, touches his arm affectionately and turns to walk away. As she does so a pile of jeering faces appear from behind the rocks where they've been hiding and listening

Susan (*turning back*) Clear off, all of you. Go and play football or something. I said go!

Reilly's followers move away a little

Brian.

She motions him to join her. He does

You know what I was saying about leagues? Well have you ever thought about whose league Linda's in?

Reilly Linda Croxley? She doesn't fancy me. She's mad about Sir. No-one else can get a look in.

Susan I wouldn't be too sure about that.

Song 13: I Know You Like Her

(*Singing*)   I know you like her
                    Yes you do, you know you do
                    I can't be sure but
                    I think that she likes you.

Reilly Ah go way Miss. You're nuts.

Susan   Maybe, if you asked her
                    Out one night, she'd like to go
                    Anyway, no harm done
                    The worst thing she can say is "no".

Reilly No chance.

Susan   Perhaps you think you'd never ever stand a
                        chance with her
                    Maybe never ever get a second glance from her
                    So where the hell's your confidence
                    All you need's a bit of nerve

Reilly I'm no good at . . .

Susan   Don't put yourself down
                    Can't you see you're not so bad
                    (*She gives him her compact mirror from her
                        handbag*)
                    Take a look at your reflection
                    There you'll see a handsome lad

Reilly is smiling and flattered

                    Perhaps you think you'd never stand a chance
                        with her
                    Maybe never even get a second glance from her
                    So where the hell's your confidence
                    All you need's a bit of nerve.

                    I know you like her
                    Yes you do, you know you do
                    I can't be sure but
                    I think that she likes you (*repeating*) She likes
                        you.

Susan See you, Brian.

Reilly See y', Miss.

*He turns and walks to his mates. They begin jeering and laughing but
he stands smiling and proud*

   Well! At least I'm not like you ugly gets. *I* am handsome!

There are more jeers

The Driver, Mrs Kay and the footballers rush on playing

Reilly and the others join the game. As Reilly scores Mrs Kay gives up being goalie

Mrs Kay Whoooh. I've had enough, I'm all in.
Maurice Ah Miss, we've got no goalie now.

Susan and Colin approach the group

Mrs Kay Carol can go in goal. (*To Susan and Colin*) Where is she?
Susan Who?

The Kids all exit

Mrs Kay Carol. I thought she was with you.
Colin We haven't seen her for hours.
Mrs Kay I thought ... You haven't seen her at all?
Susan We thought she was here.
Mrs Kay (*looking around*) Oh, she couldn't, could she?
Susan Lost?
Mrs Kay Don't say it. Perhaps he's seen her. (*Shouting off to Briggs*) Mr Briggs ... Mr Briggs ...

Briggs enters

Briggs Is that it then? Are we going home?
Mrs Kay Have you seen Carol Chandler in the last hour?
Briggs I thought I'd made it quite plain that I was having nothing more to do with your outing.
Mrs Kay Have you seen Carol Chandler?
Briggs No, I haven't.
Mrs Kay I think she may have wandered off somewhere.
Briggs You mean you've lost her?
Mrs Kay No. I mean she might have wandered off somewhere!
Briggs Well what's that if it's not losing her? All I can say is it's a wonder you haven't lost half a dozen of them. (*He turns to go*)
Colin Listen, Briggs, it's about time someone told you what a berk you ...
Briggs (*wheeling on him*) And you listen! Sonny! Don't you try to tell me a thing, because you haven't even earned the right. Don't you worry, when we get back to school your number's up, as well as hers (*Indicating Mrs Kay*). And you (*indicating Susan*).

Yes. I saw what was going on between you and Reilly. When we get back I'll have the lot of you.

Mrs Kay Would you mind postponing your threats until we find Carol Chandler. At the moment I'd say the most important thing is to find the girl.

Briggs Don't you mean *try* and find her.

Mrs Kay Susan, you keep the rest of them playing football. We'll split up and look for her.

They go off in separate directions

We see Carol. She is standing on a cliff, looking out, waving at seagulls

Song 14: Why Can't It Always Be This Way

Carol (*singing*) Why can't it always be this way?
Why can't it last for more than just a day?
The sun in the sky and the seagulls flying by
I think I'd like to stay
then it could always be this way

Why can't it always be like this?
I can't think of anything back home that I
would miss
Suppose there'd be a fuss if I wasn't on the
bus?
But it really would be bliss
If it could always be like this

Shouting to the seagulls,
Seagulls say "hello"
Wonder how they stay up there so high
Looking at the seashore miles and miles
below
Makes me wish that I could fly

Why can't we just stay where we are?
Far far away from the muck and motor cars
If I close my eyes and try and try and try
And wish upon a star,
Then we could all just stay where we are.

As the song ends, Briggs appears on the cliffs and sees Carol

Briggs Carol Chandler, just come here. Who gave you permission to come on these cliffs?

Carol (*moving to the edge*) No-one. (*She turns, dismissing him*)

Briggs I'm talking to you, Miss Chandler.

Carol continues to ignore his presence

Now just listen here, young lady. . . .

Carol (*suddenly turning*) Don't you come near me!

Briggs (*taken aback by her vehemence he stops*) Pardon.

Carol I don't want you to come near me.

Briggs Well in that case just get yourself moving and let's get down to the beach.

Carol You go. *I'm* not comin'.

Briggs You what?

Carol Tell Mrs Kay she can go home without me. I'm stoppin' here, by the sea.

Pause

Briggs Now you just listen to me. I've had just about enough today, just about enough and I'm not putting up with a pile of silliness from the likes of you. Now come on!

He starts towards her but she moves to the very edge of the cliff

Carol Try an' get me an' I'll jump over.

Briggs is stopped in his tracks, astounded and angered

Briggs (*shouting*) Listen, you stupid girl, get yourself over here, this minute.

Carol ignores him

I'll not tell you again!

They stare at each other. It's obvious that she will not do as he bids

Briggs I'll give you five seconds! Just five seconds. one, two, three, four—I'm warning you!—five.

Carol I've told y', I'm not comin' with y'. I *will* jump y' know. I will.

Briggs Just what are you tryin' to do to me?

Carol I've told y', just leave me alone an' I won't jump. (*Pause*) I wanna stay here where it's nice.

Briggs Stay here? How could you stay here? What would you do eh? Where would you live?

Carol I'd be all right.

Briggs I've told you, stop being silly.

Carol (*turning on him*) What are you worried for eh? You don't care do y'? Do y'?

Briggs What? About you? Listen, if I didn't care, why would I be up here now, trying to stop you doing something stupid?

Carol Because if I jumped over, you'd get into trouble when you get back to school. That's why, Briggsy, so stop goin' on. You hate me.

Briggs Don't be ridiculous. Just because I'm a schoolteacher it doesn't mean to say that——

Carol Don't lie you! I know you hate me. I've seen you goin' home in your car, passin' us on the street. An' the way you look at us. You hate all the kids.

Briggs What . . . Why do you say that?

Carol Why can't I just stay out here an' live in one of them nice white houses, an' do the garden an' that?

Briggs Look—Carol. You're talking as though you've given up on life. It sounds as though life for you is ending, instead of just beginning. Now why can't . . . I mean, if that's what you want . . . why can't . . . what's to stop you working hard at school from now on, getting a good job and then moving out here when you're old enough? Eh?

Carol (*she turns and looks at him with pure contempt*) Don't be so bloody stupid. (*She turns and looks out to the sea*) It's been a great day today. I loved it. I don't wanna leave here an' go home. (*Pause*) If I stayed it wouldn't be any good though, would it? You'd send the coppers to get me, wouldn't y'?

Briggs We'd have to. How would you survive out here?

Carol I know. (*Pause*) I'm not goin' back though. (*She kneels at the cliff edge and looks over*)

Briggs Carol, please.

Carol Sir, you know if you'd been my old feller—I would've been all right wouldn't I?

Briggs slowly and cautiously creeps forward, holding out his hand

Briggs Carol, please come away from there.

Carol looks down over the cliff

Please.

Carol Sir, sir you don't half look funny y' know.
Briggs (*smiling*) Why?
Carol Sir, you should smile more often. You look great when y' smile.
Briggs (*holding out his hand*) Come on, Carol.
Carol Sir—what'll happen to me for doin' this?
Briggs Nothing. I promise.
Carol Sir, you're promisin' now, but what about back at school?
Briggs It won't even be mentioned, I promise.

His hand is outstretched. She decides to believe him and reaches out for his hand. As she does she slips but he manages to lunge forward and clasp her to safety. He stands with his arms wrapped around her

The other Kids are playing football. Reilly with the ball is trying to get past a huge row of defenders

Linda (*from the side of the game*) Go on, Brian, go on, go on. . . .

Reilly scores

Yes!

Reilly preens himself for Linda

Mrs Kay enters with Susan, shaking her head

Mrs Kay I think we'd better let the police know.
Susan Shall I keep them playing?

Briggs and Carol join the group

Oh, he's found her.
Colin I'll bet he makes a bloody meal out of this.
Susan It doesn't matter. She's safe, that's the main thing.
Colin We'd better round them up. It'll be straight home now.

Colin begins to get the Kids together

Mrs Kay (*approaching Briggs and Carol*) Carol where were you?
Carol On the cliff, Miss.
Mrs Kay On the . . .
Briggs It's all right, Mrs Kay, we've been through all that. Now. If you'll just let me deal with this.

Mrs Kay puts her arm around Carol

Mrs Kay Carol! The worry you've caused. Oh, love.
Briggs Come on. Everyone on the coach.

Driver Back to the school then?

Briggs School? Back to school? It's still early isn't it? Anyway—
you can't come all the way to the seaside and not pay a visit to
the fair.

Music introduction for Song 15 starts

Carol (*rushing to the other Kids*) We're goin' the fair, Sir's takin'
us to the fair.

Briggs turns to Mrs Kay who still can't believe her ears

Briggs You never know Mrs Kay—play your cards right an' I
might take you for a ride on the waltzer!

*The benches are formed into a circle to represent a waltzer on to
which everyone piles*

Song 15: Fairground Song

All (*singing*)

> We're goin on the waltzer
> We're gonna have some fun
> Gonna get dead dizzy
> Gonna get well spun
> Hold your belly, gasp for air
> Ooh! Ooh feel the wind in your hair
>
> Sir's on the waltzer
> He's takin' us to the fair
>
> We're goin' on the dodgems
> And on the ferris wheel
> Going on the ghost train
> Gonna giggle and scream
> Don't know who's scared the most
> Digga or Reilly or the bleedin' ghost
>
> Sir's on the dodgems
> He's takin' us to the fair
>
> We've never seen him laugh before
> He's not like this in school
> It must be something in the air
> That makes him play the fool
>
> Candy floss and hot dogs
> Gonna get real sick
> Look at old Briggsy

> In a kiss-me-quick
> Big dipper? Yes, sir, please
> Hold on everybody now
> Say cheese ...

Everybody forms into a group for Mrs Kay's camera, holding the note on the word "cheese". A cowboy hat is produced for Briggs to wear. In this pause the two bored girls are apart from the rest of the group

Bored 1 What d' y' think?
Bored 2 The fair?
Bored 1 Yeh.
Bored 2 (*considering*) Borin'!

Everybody leaps back on to the waltzer

> Sirs's on the waltzer
> He's takin' us to the fair

Repeat the middle eight

Repeat the final verse

There is a big finish on the last line, ending with Briggs being lifted on to shoulders by a group of Kids and being photographed by Mrs Kay

Briggs Last one on the coach pays the fare.

The Kids sing without accompaniment as they re-form the coach

Song 16: Everywhere We Go

Kids (*singing*)
> Everywhere we go
> Everywhere we go
> People wanna know
> People wanna know
> Who we are
> Who we are
> So we tell them
> So we tell them
> We are the Progress
> The mighty, mighty Progress

The coach is now re-formed and nearly everyone is on board. Ronson runs up to the coach and Briggs who is standing waiting for him

Ronson Sir, that was great that, it was great.
Briggs Come on.
Ronson Sir, can we come again tomorrow?
Briggs Oh, get on the bus, Ronson.

Piano underscore – "She'll Be Coming Round the Mountain"

The Kids on the coach are now mostly asleep or dozing. Briggs, wearing the cowboy hat, makes his way along the aisle. When he reaches Mrs Kay she turns the camera on him and takes a snapshot. It is as if in that moment the flashlight signals the beginning of a return to reality for Mr Briggs. He becomes conscious of the hat he is wearing and, smiling at Mrs Kay, removes it and places it on the head of the sleeping Carol, who is clutching a fairground goldfish. Mrs Kay puts the completed film into a canister. Briggs walks down the aisle

Briggs (*to Mrs Kay*) Well … nearly home.
Mrs Kay (*indicating the film*) I've got some gems of you in here. We'll have one of these put up in the staff room when they're developed.
Briggs Eh? One of me? What for?
Mrs Kay Don't worry, I'm not going to let you forget the day you enjoyed yourself.
Briggs (*watching her put the canister into an envelope*) Look. Erm … why don't you let me develop those? I could do them in the lab.
Mrs Kay I don't know—using school facilities for personal gain. (*She hands over the film*) Thank you.
Briggs Have them done as soon as I can. (*He sits down*)
Linda (*to Reilly*) Are y' glad y' came?
Reilly Yeh.
Linda It was great, wasn't it eh?
Reilly It'll be the last trip I go on.
Linda Why?
Reilly Well I'm leavin' in the Summer aren't I?
Linda What y'gonna do?
Reilly Nothin' I suppose … (*He looks out of the window*) It's bleedin' horrible when y' look at it isn't it?
Linda What?
Reilly (*nodding, indicating the city*) That. Liverpool.
Linda Yeh.

Underscoring ends as the coach stops

Briggs Right. Come on, everybody off.

During the following all the seats of the coach are removed

Song 16a: We Had A Really Great Day Out

Kids (*singing*)	We had a really great day out
	We went to the beach and went daft and ran about
	We went to the zoo
	And the fair and castle too
	And Briggsy let us sing and shout
	Coming back from our day out

Briggs (*speaking*) OK. Everybody off.

Driver	That's the end of that one, see y' all take care
	Better get off home now to me wife
	Out tomorrow morning
	No idea where
	It's a funny way of life
Kids (*singing*)	Thanks, Ron, we had a lovely day
	Thanks, Sir and Miss, it was cracker, Mrs Kay
	The best we ever had
	Even Briggsy's not so bad
	Never seen him act that way
	He must have had a lovely day
	Climbing off the bus now
	Back in Liverpool
	Better get off home now for me tea
	Looking at the streets, the playground and the school,
	Seems a long way from the sea

Continue melody as underscoring

Everybody is now off the coach. The Driver and various Kids have moved off. Reilly and Linda, arms around each other, pass Mr Briggs

Reilly Night, Sir. Enjoyed yourself today didn't y', Sir.

Briggs Pardon.
Reilly I didn't know you was like that, Sir. All right for a laugh an'
  that. See y' tomorrow, Sir.

Briggs nods goodbye to them and then suddenly calls after them

Briggs Oh—Linda.

She stops and turns

  We, erm … we'll let the uniform go this time. But don't let me
  catch you dressing like that again on a school outing.

  Reilly and Linda exit

Bored 1 Wasn't that a great day?
Bored 2 It was cracker. Come on.

  The two bored girls run off

Mrs Kay Well that seems to be it. (*She sees Carol hovering
  nearby*.) Are you going home Carol?

  From off we hear a whistle and the Driver enters

Driver Erm, excuse me madam, have you lost a small python?
Mrs Kay (*just for a second thinking, as do we, that it might be
  true*) What!

*From behind his back the Driver produces the goldfish in the plastic
bag*

Driver (*as he hands it to Carol*) They always forget somethin'.
Mrs Kay Thanks, Ronny.
Driver Thanks Helen. Goodnight. (*To others as he exits*) 'Bye
  now. See y'.

  The Driver exits

Colin ⎫
Susan ⎬ (*together*) Goodnight.
Briggs ⎭

Mrs Kay Well, that's that. I don't know about anyone else but I'm
  for a drink.
Susan Oh, I'll second that.
Colin They'll just be open.
Mrs Kay (*to Briggs*) You going to join us?

Briggs Oh, well actually I've …
Susan Oh come on.
Briggs No, I'd er … I'd better not. Thanks anyway. I've got lots of
marking to do at home. Thanks all the same.
Mrs Kay Well if we can't twist your arm—thanks for today.

*Mrs Kay turns and leads the others off, failing to see Carol hovering
in the shadows*

Car's over here.

Mrs Kay, Colin and Susan exit

*Briggs reaches into his pocket for his car keys. Along with the keys
he brings out the package containing the film. He stands, looking at
the package unaware of:*

*The Kids, Reilly, Andrews, Jackie, Carol, Digga, Maurice,
Ronson, Milton, Linda, Little Kid, Boring Girls and every other
one of them, appear individually from behind him and watch him*

*Carol walks forward out of the shadows as Briggs suddenly makes
his decision and exposes the role of film. He turns and sees Carol
watching him along with all the other kids. Carol moves off as if to go
home. From off we hear:*

Parent Carol! Where've you been? Just get in this bloody house.

Song: No-One Can Take This Time Away
(set to tune of No.14)

Kids No-one can take this time away
No matter what they cannot take the day
No-one can steal
Something you just feel
And although the picture fades
No-one can take this time away

(*note double middle eight*)

Someone said the pictures
Just didn't turn out right
Someone said the shutter had been closed
Someone said the camera
Was pointing at the light
And the film had been exposed

But who needs a picture
Pictures always fade
Just get lost or stuck behind a drawer
And I can always find
A picture in my mind
Of some far distant shore

No-one can take this time away
No matter what they do no matter what they say
We couldn't give a toss

(*spoken*) 'cos it was:

"Brilliant"
            "magic"
                        "boss"!

And although the picture fades

But instead of it being the last line of this verse, the following becomes the first *line of a reprised first verse*

All   No-one can take this time away
No matter what they cannot take the day
No-one can steal
Something you just feel
And although the picture fades
No-one can take this time away.

CURTAIN

FURNITURE AND PROPERTY LIST

Only essential properties, as listed in the script, are given here. Further items and dressing can be added at the producer's discretion

On stage: Chairs/Benches

Off stage: Sweets **(Kid)**
Tea and cakes **(Stage Management)**
Animals, including a hen **(Kids)**
Football **(Driver)**
Cowboy Hat **(Briggs)**
Goldfish in plastic bag **(Carol)**

Personal: **Kids:** sweets, chocolates, lemonade
Driver: money
Reilly: cigarettes
Mrs Kay: handbag. *In it:* camera. Shopping bag. *In it:* Flask of coffee
Susan: handbag. *In it:* mirror
Les: "lollipop" sign

LIGHTING PLOT

Only essential cues, as given in the script, are listed here. Other effects may
be added as required

ACT I

To open: Daylight

Cue 1	At end of "packed lunch" round *Black-out. Lights up on Head's study*	(Page 3)
Cue 2	**Briggs:** ". . . go with her, won't I?" *Black-out study. Lights up on coach*	(Page 4)
Cue 3	As coach goes into tunnel *Black-out. Lights up when ready*	(Page 17)
Cue 4	**Shopkeeper:** ". . . you can get out". *Black-out shop area. Lights on shop exterior*	(Page 22)
Cue 5	**Briggs:** ". . . looking after them." *Black-out on teachers. Lights up on shop area*	(Page 22)
Cue 6	**Shopkeeper:** "NO!" *Black-out on shop. Lights up on teacher*	(Page 23)
Cue 7	**Briggs:** "ANIMALS." *Black-out*	(Page 23)

ACT II

To open: Exterior lighting

Cue 8	**Parent:** ". . . in this bloody house!" *Black-out*	(Page 55)

EFFECTS PLOT

Only essential effects, as given in the script, are listed here. Further effects
can be added as required

Cue 1	**Kids** (*singing*) "What's over on the other side?" *Sound of the ocean*	(Page 41)

MADE AND PRINTED IN GREAT BRITAIN BY
LATIMER TREND & COMPANY LTD PLYMOUTH

MADE IN ENGLAND